# Fantasy and Fairytale
# CHARACTERS

Grayscale Coloring Book
by Christine Karron

This coloring book is designed for experienced colorists and beginners as well. Recommended for coloring with markers, colored pencils, pens and/or crayons. If using wet media place a sheet of thick paper or card stock behind the coloring page to prevent bleed through. All illustrations in this book were originally created and traditionally hand drawn by the artist Christine Karron. For coloring inspirations, demo videos and more about Christine's artwork visit chkarron.com

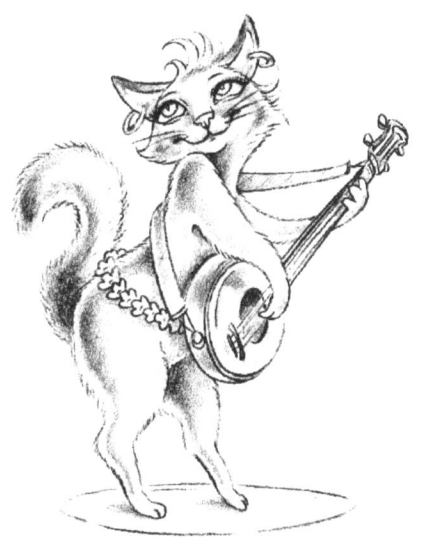

No part of this book may be reproduced or transmitted in any form or by any means, electronic or mechanical, including photocopying, recording or by any information storage and retrieval system, without written permission from the copyright holder, except for a book review.

## *Fantasy and Fairytale CHARACTERS*
Grayscale Coloring book by Christine Karron
First published August 2019

**ISBN**: 9781688932647
**Imprint**: Independently published

Copyright 2019 Christine Karron
All rights reserved
www.chkarron.com

# Fantasy and Fairytale
# CHARACTERS

Grayscale Coloring Book

1. Pirate Brielle
2. Pirate Arabella
3. Troll Girl and Fox
4. Troll Girl and Raven
5. Troll Girl Eagle Hunter
6. Viking Troll Girl with Her Dragon
7. Mermaid's Shoes
8. Mermaid's Heart
9. Jellyfish Mermaid
10. Mermaid – Enchanting Eyes
11. Mermaid's Kiss
12. Ocean's Own
13. Witch's Squad
14. Shot of Magic
15. Queen of Hearts
16. Rapunzel
17. Gypsy Girls
18. Esmeralda
19. Over the Rooftops
20. Good and Evil
21. Starborn
22. Queen of Her World
23. Scent of Spring
24. Mother's Day

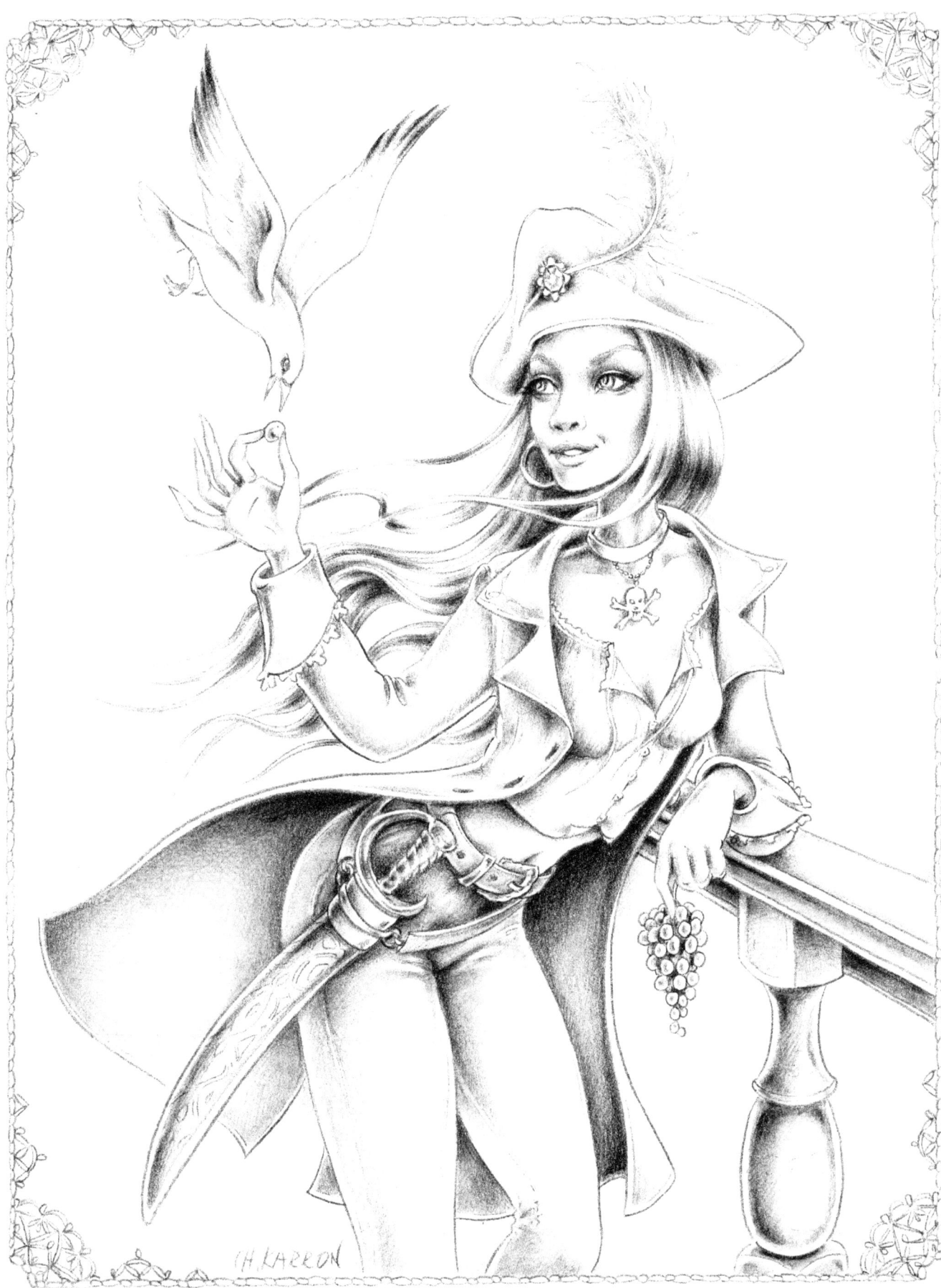

**CHARACTERS** by Christine Karron

*Pirate Brielle*

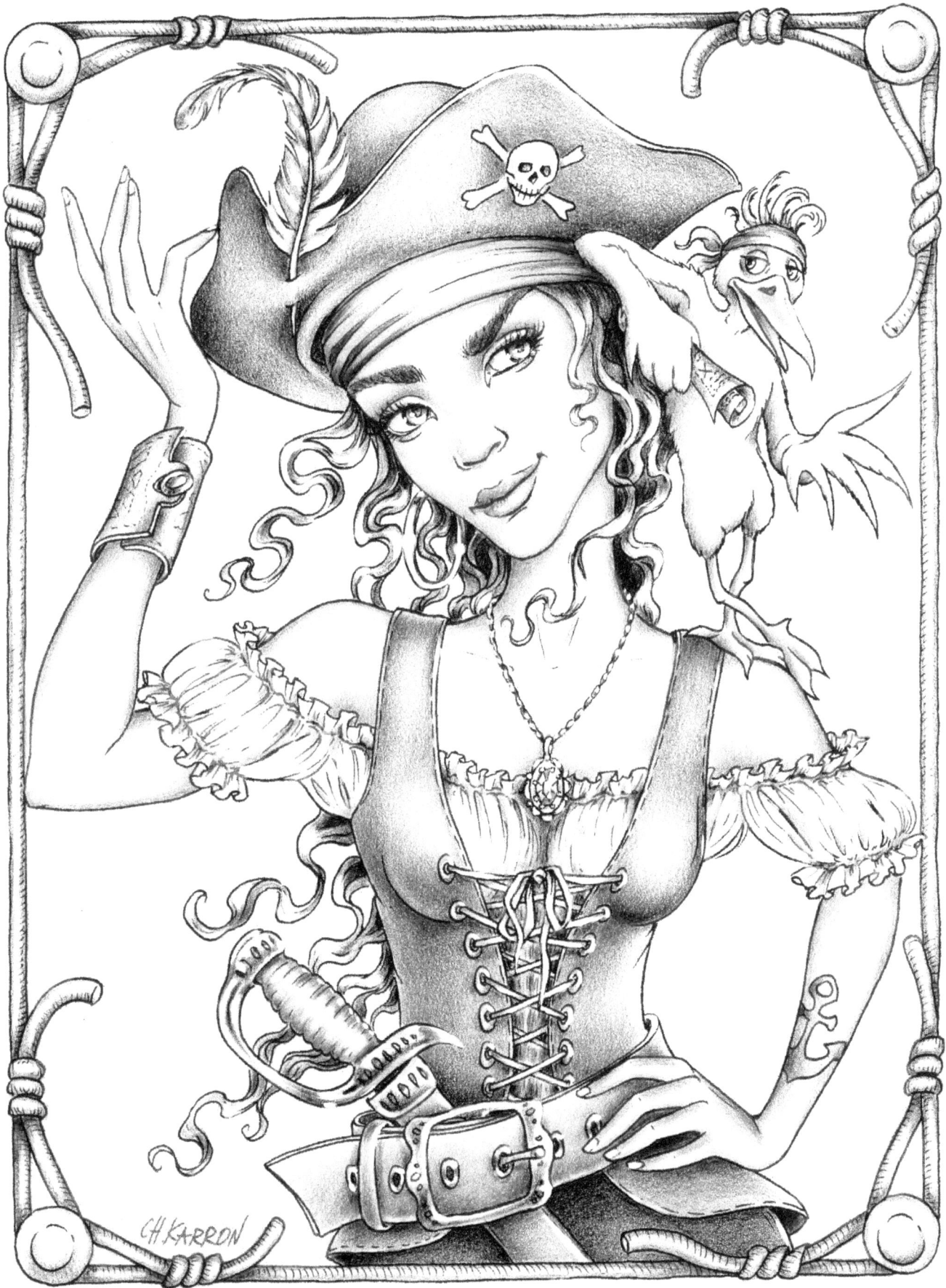

CHARACTERS by Christine Karron — Pirate Arabella

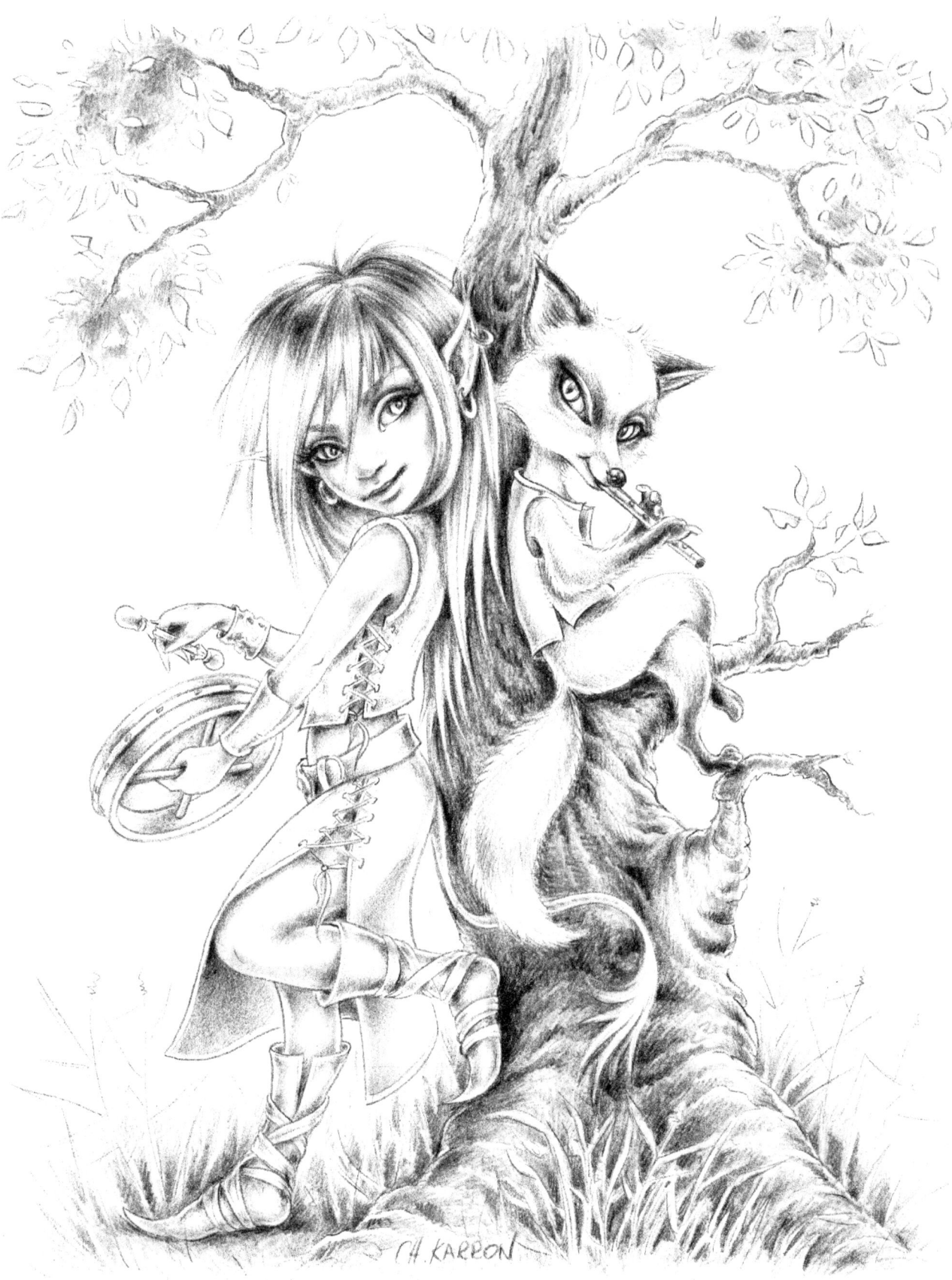

**CHARACTERS** *by Christine Karron*     *Troll Girl and Fox*

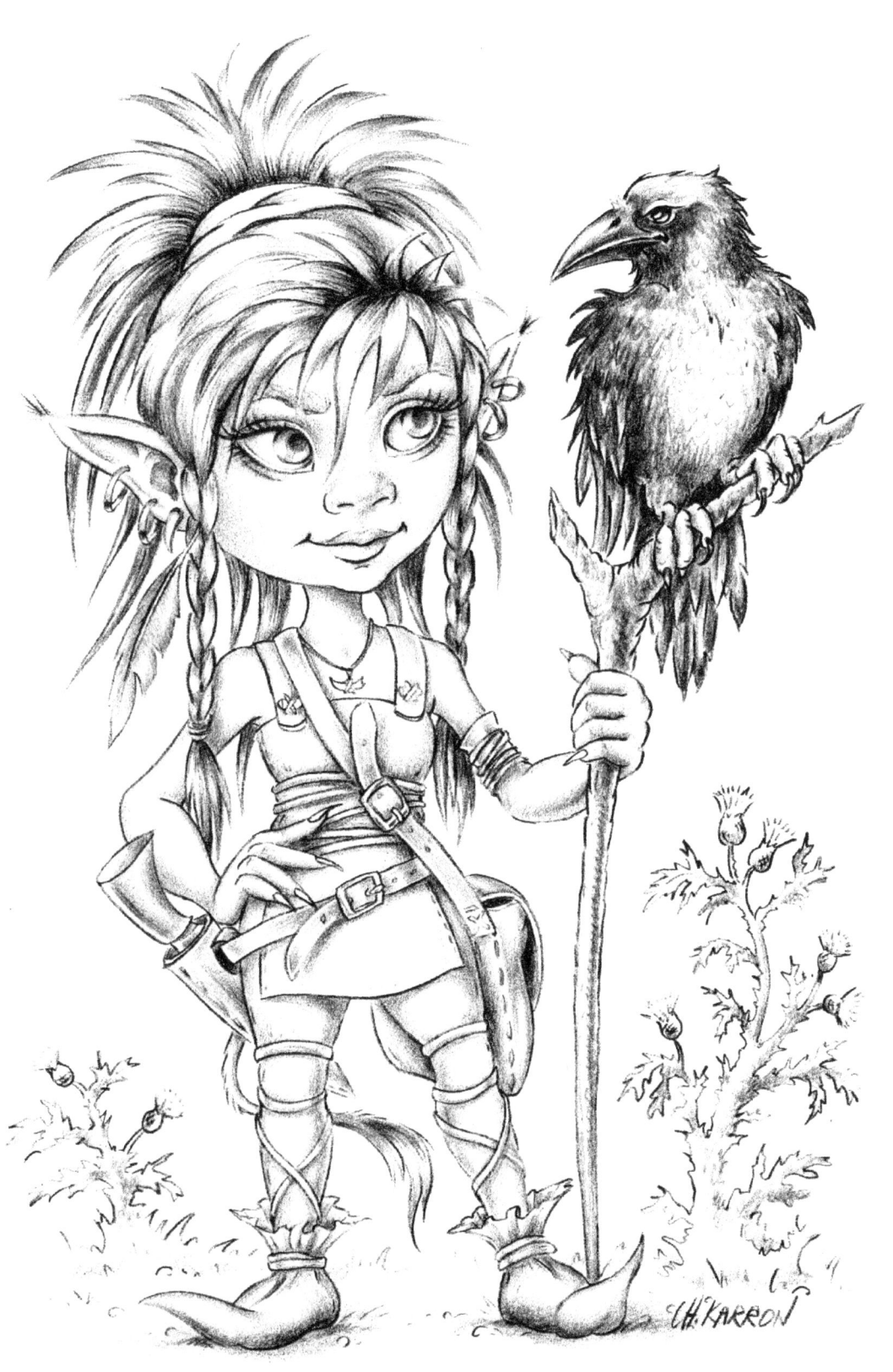

**CHARACTERS** by Christine Karron

*Troll Girl and Raven*

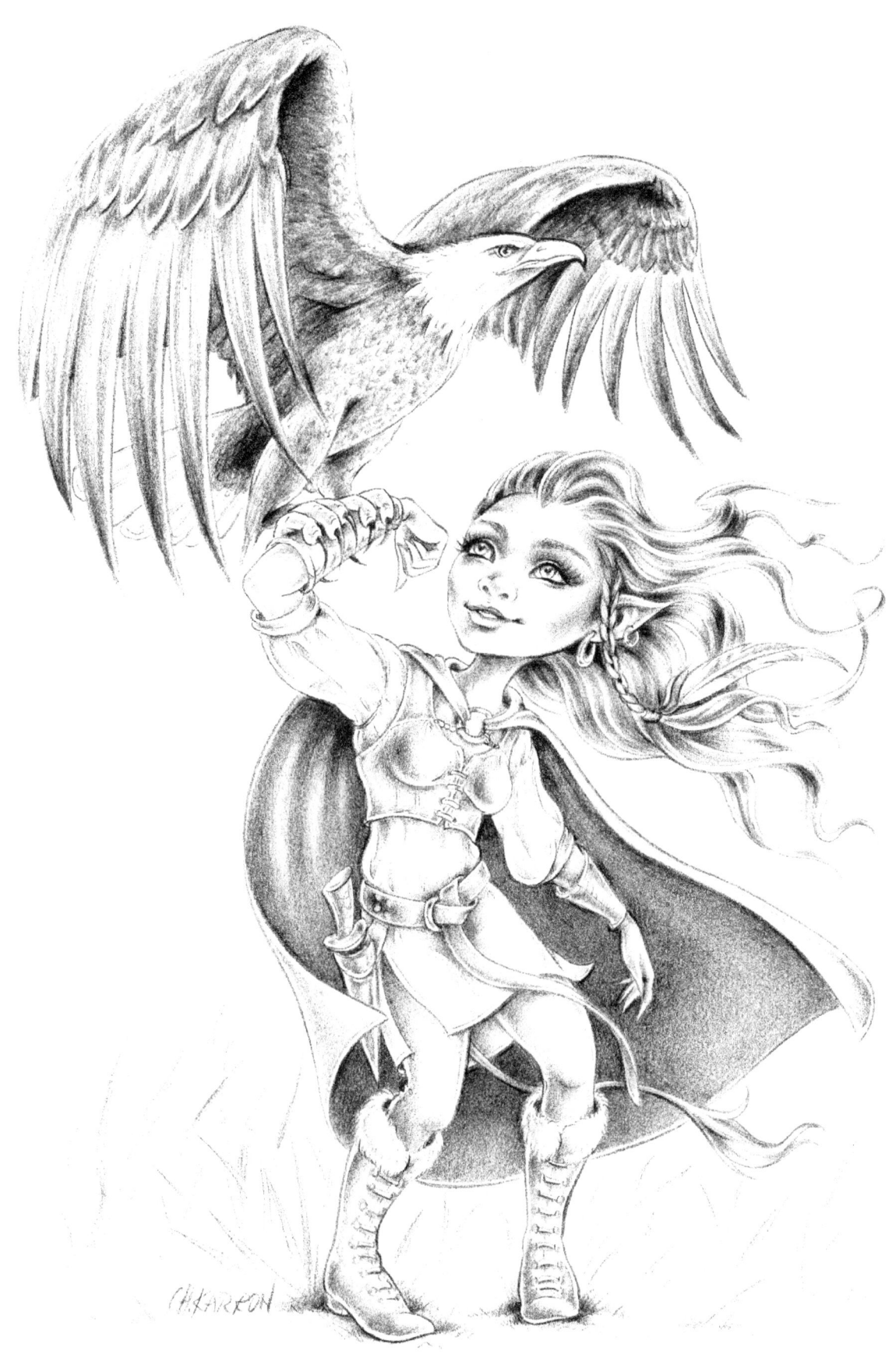

**CHARACTERS** by Christine Karron

*Troll Girl Eagle Hunter*

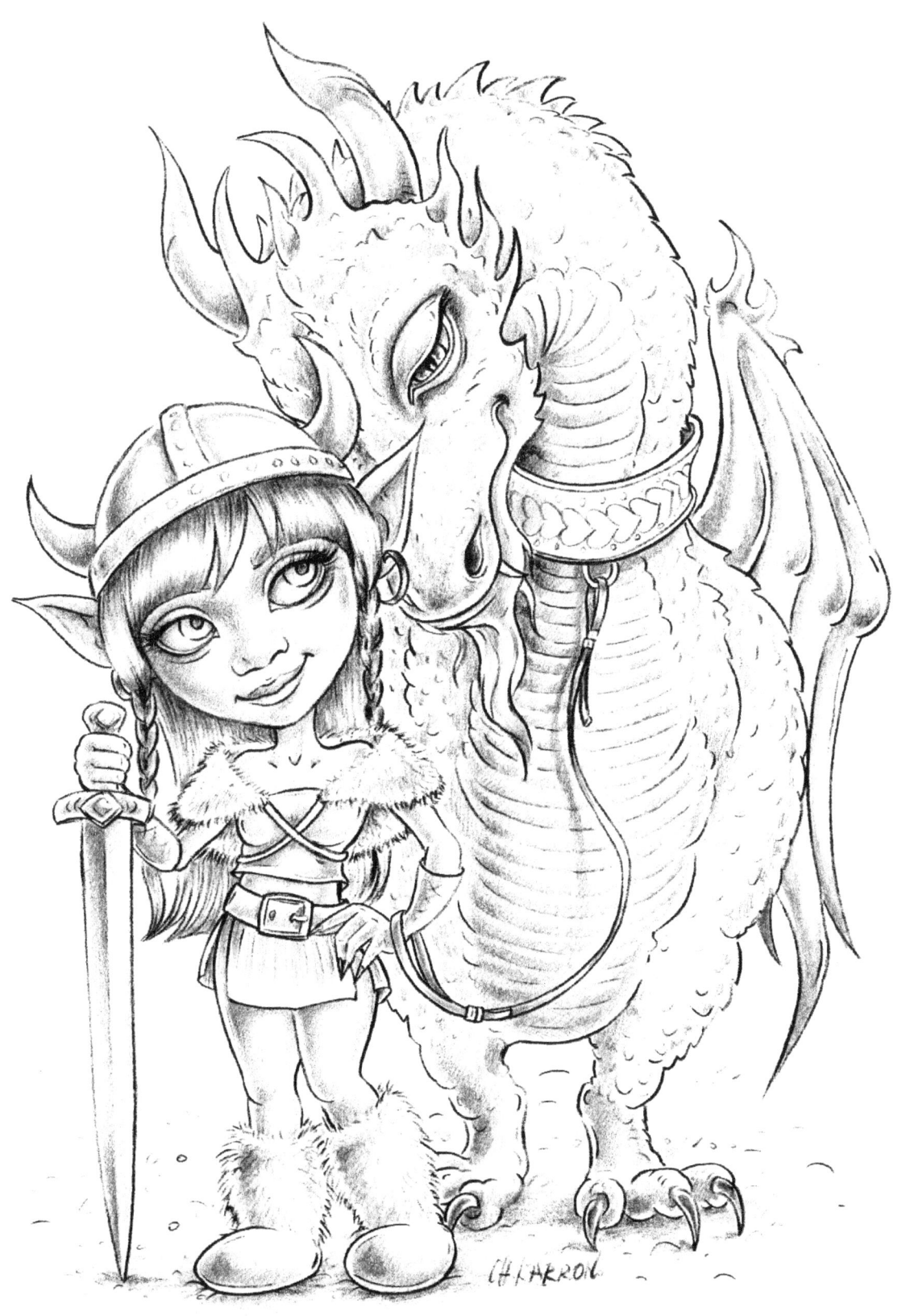

**CHARACTERS** by Christine Karron

*Viking Troll Girl with Her Dragon*

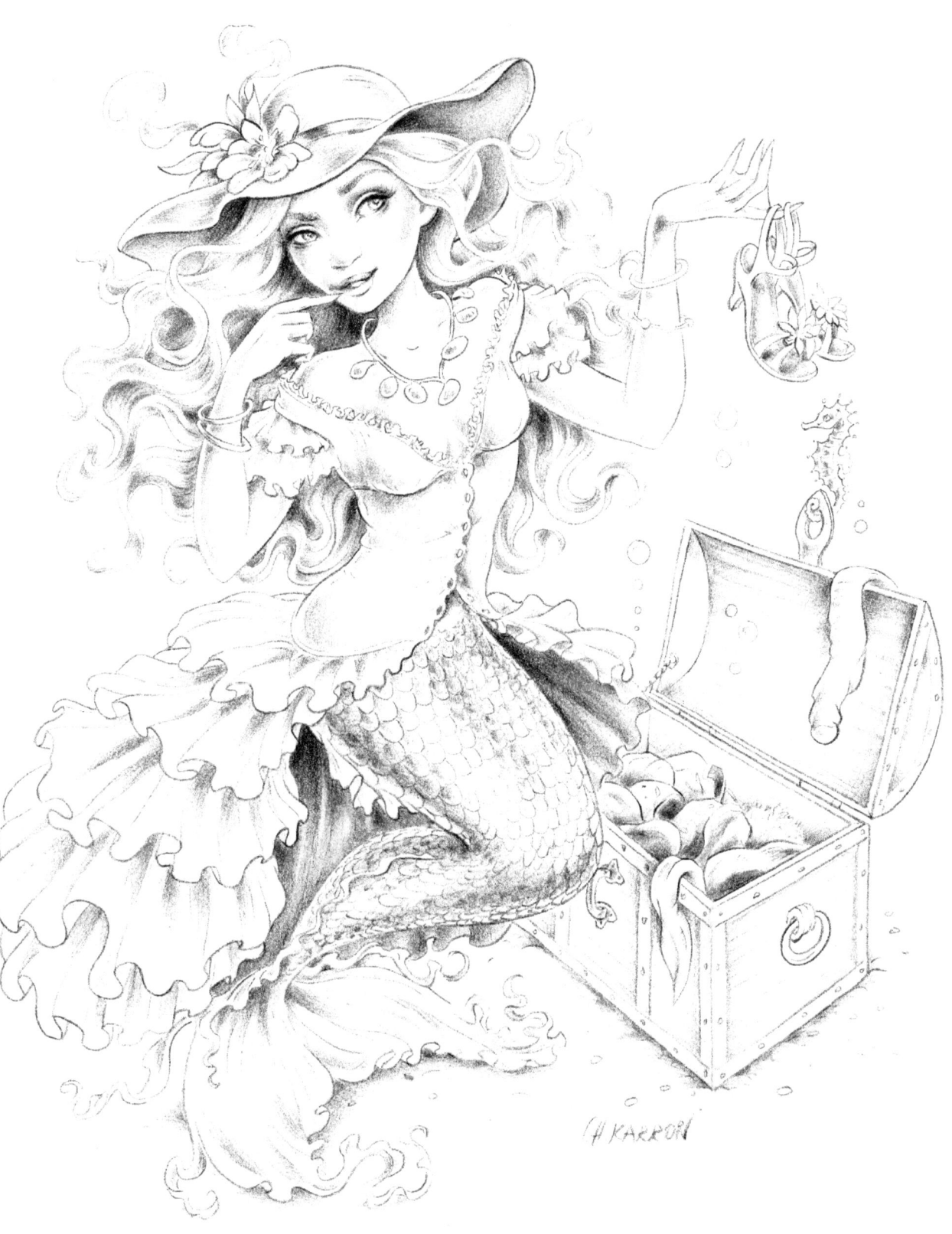

CHARACTERS  by Christine Karron

Mermaid's Shoes

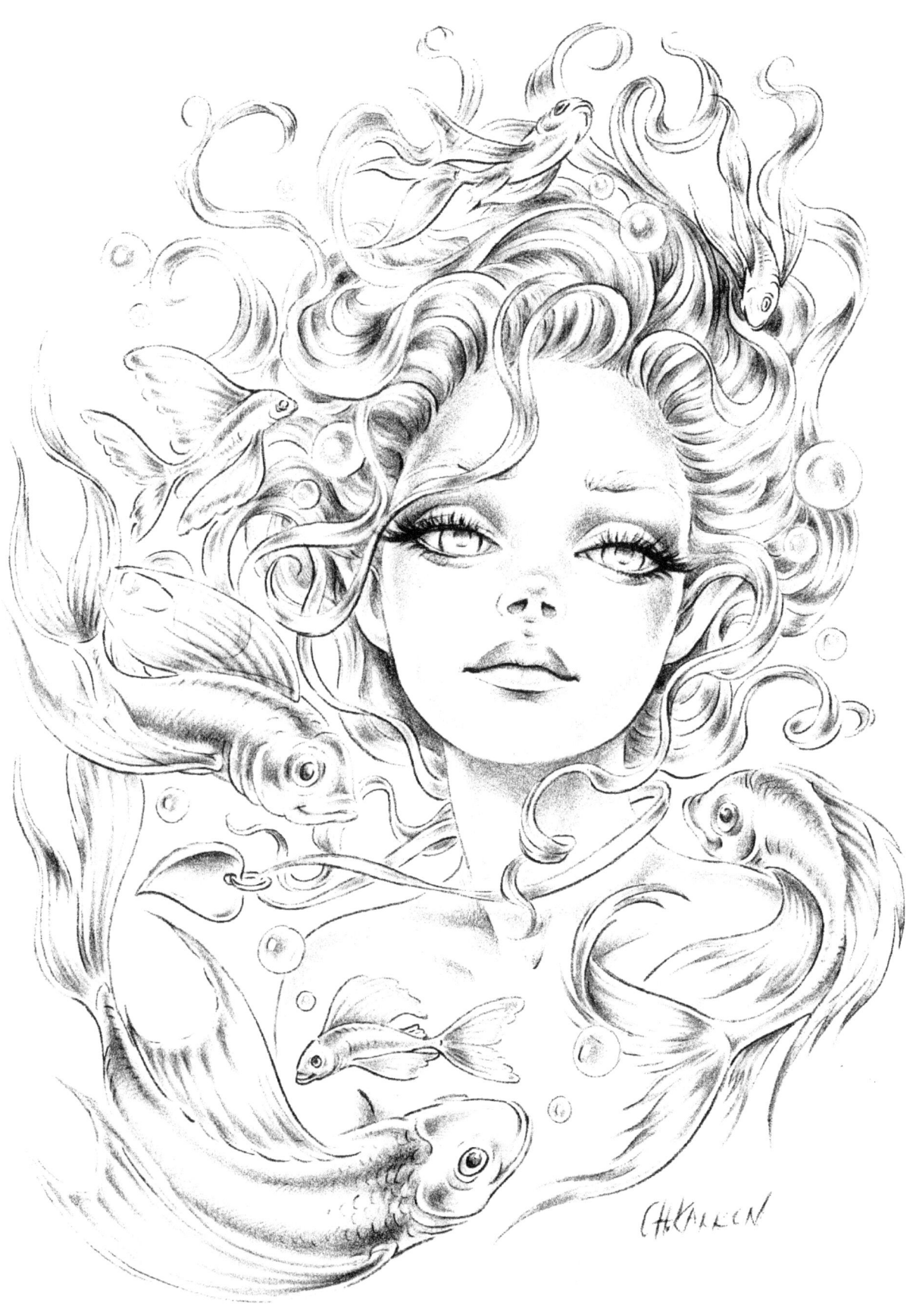

CHARACTERS by Christine Karron

Mermaid's Heart

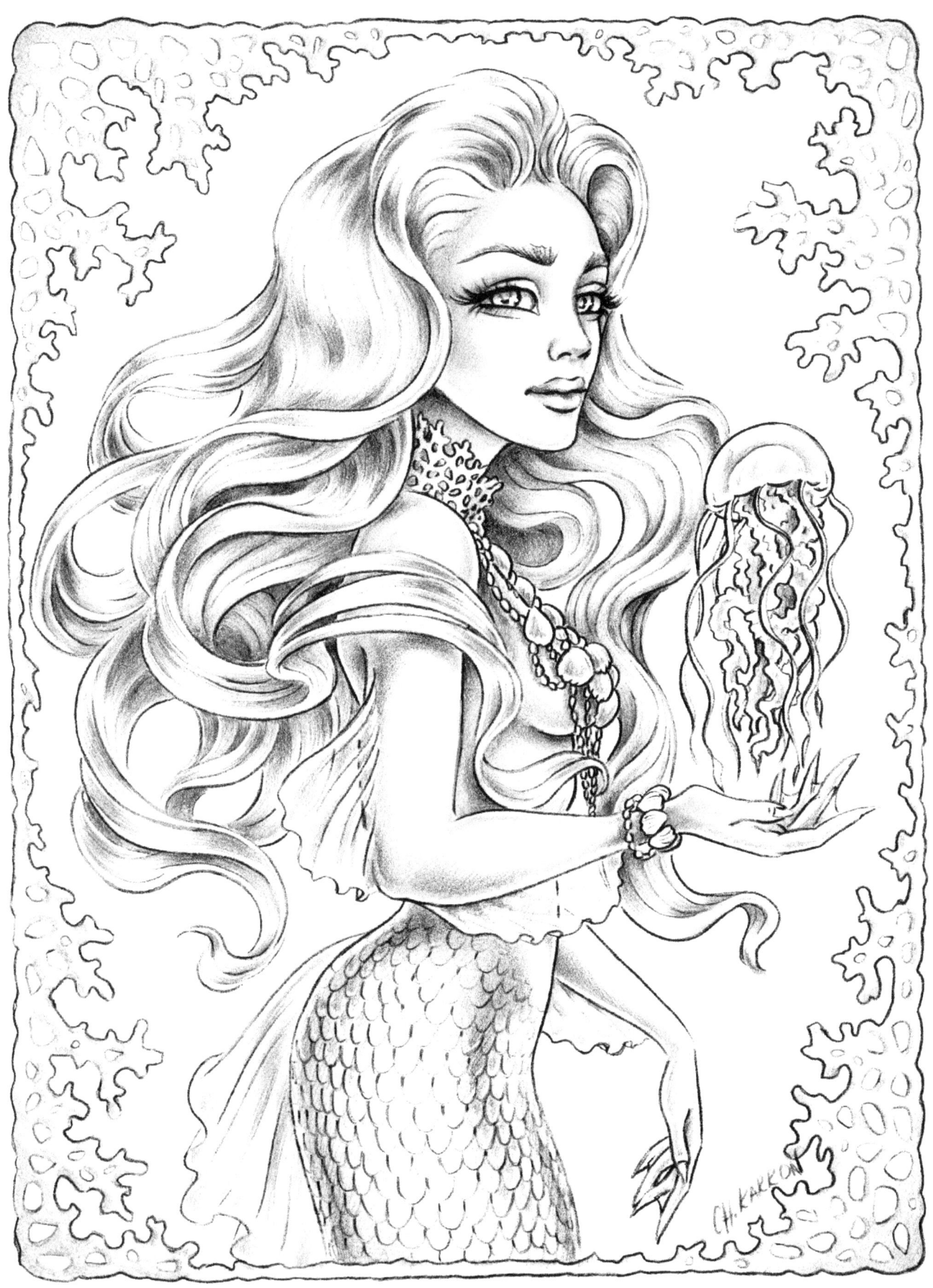

CHARACTERS by Christine Karron — Jellyfish Mermaid

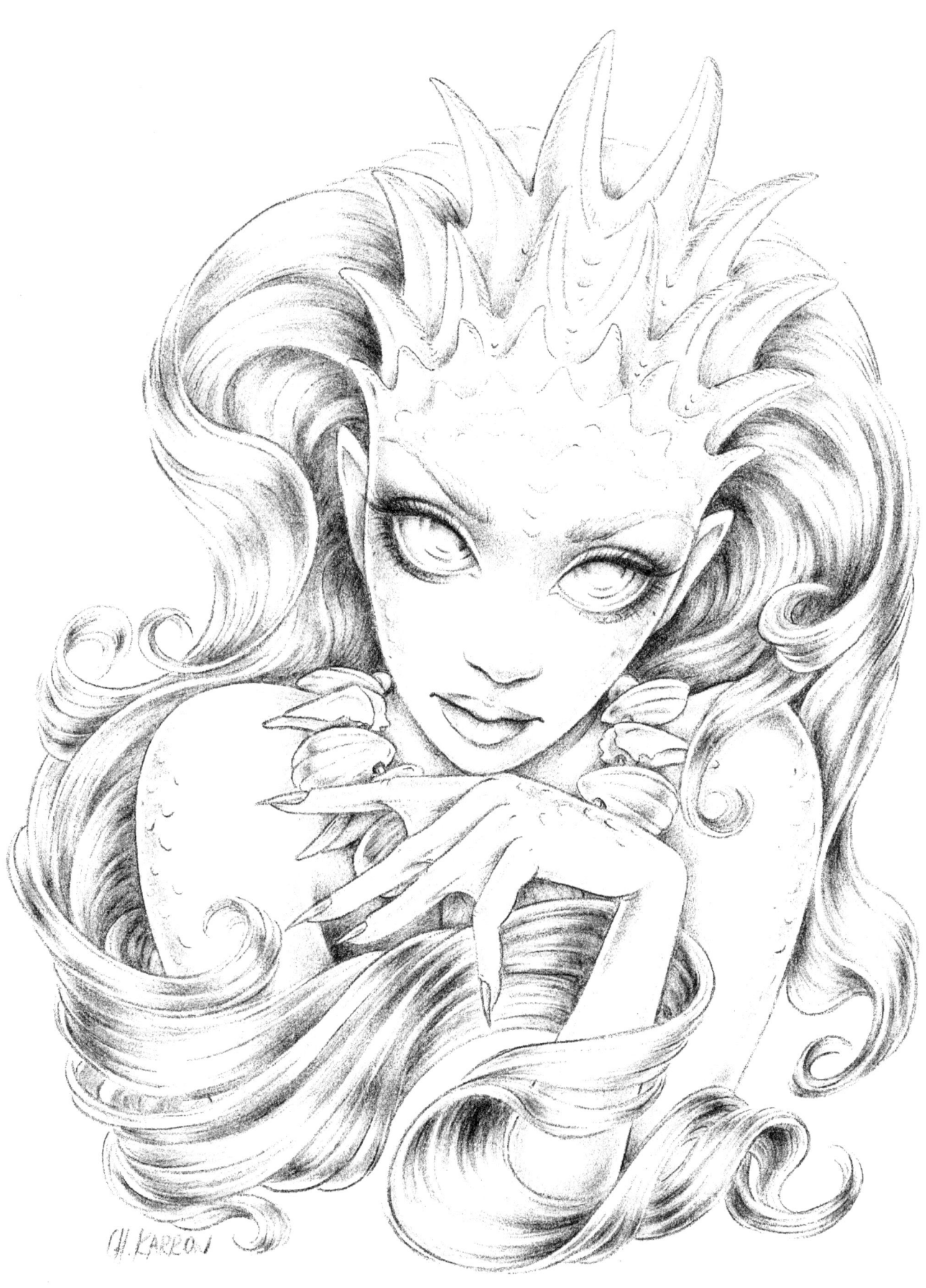

**CHARACTERS** by Christine Karron

*Mermaid - Enchanting Eyes*

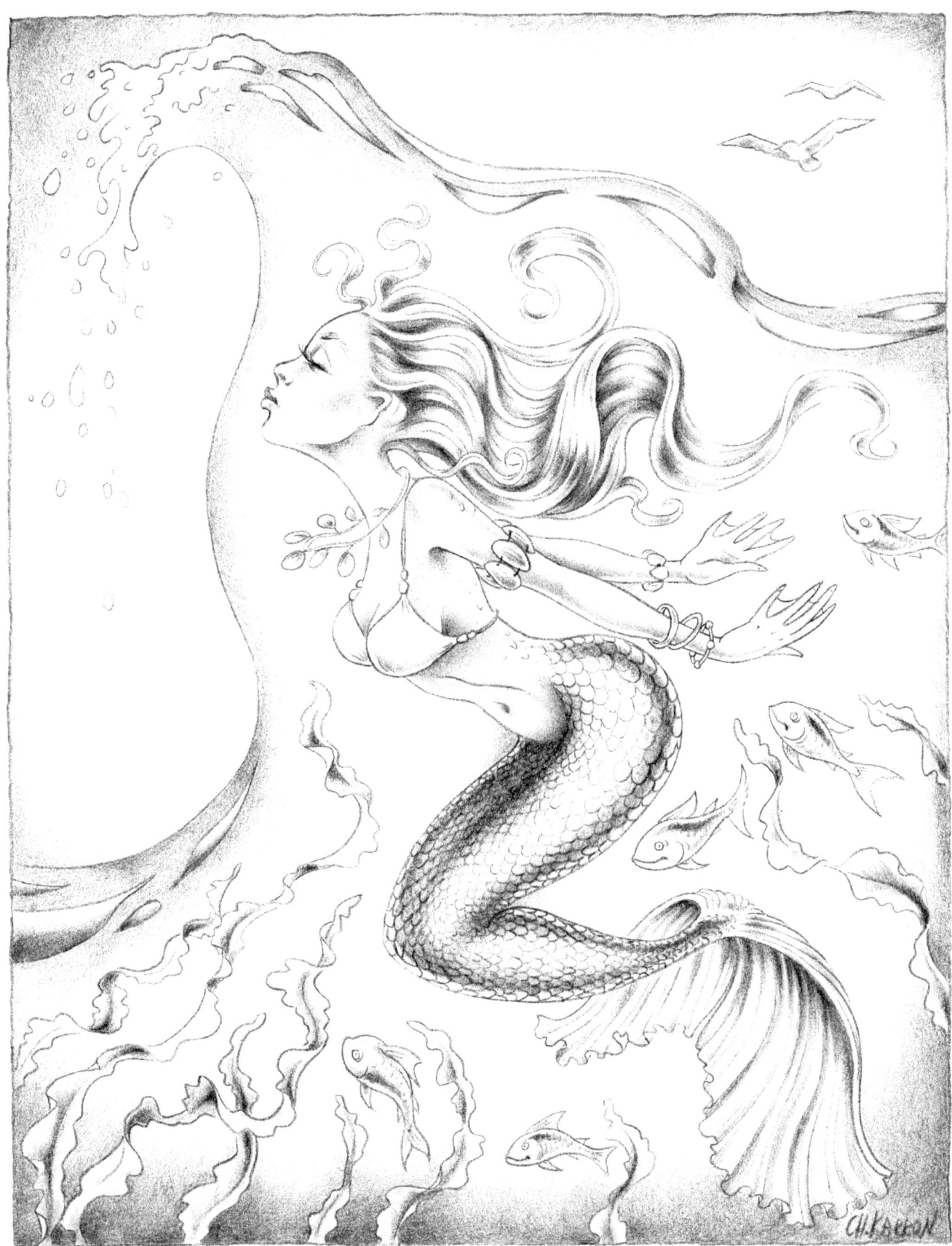

**CHARACTERS** *by Christine Karron*  *Mermaid's Kiss*

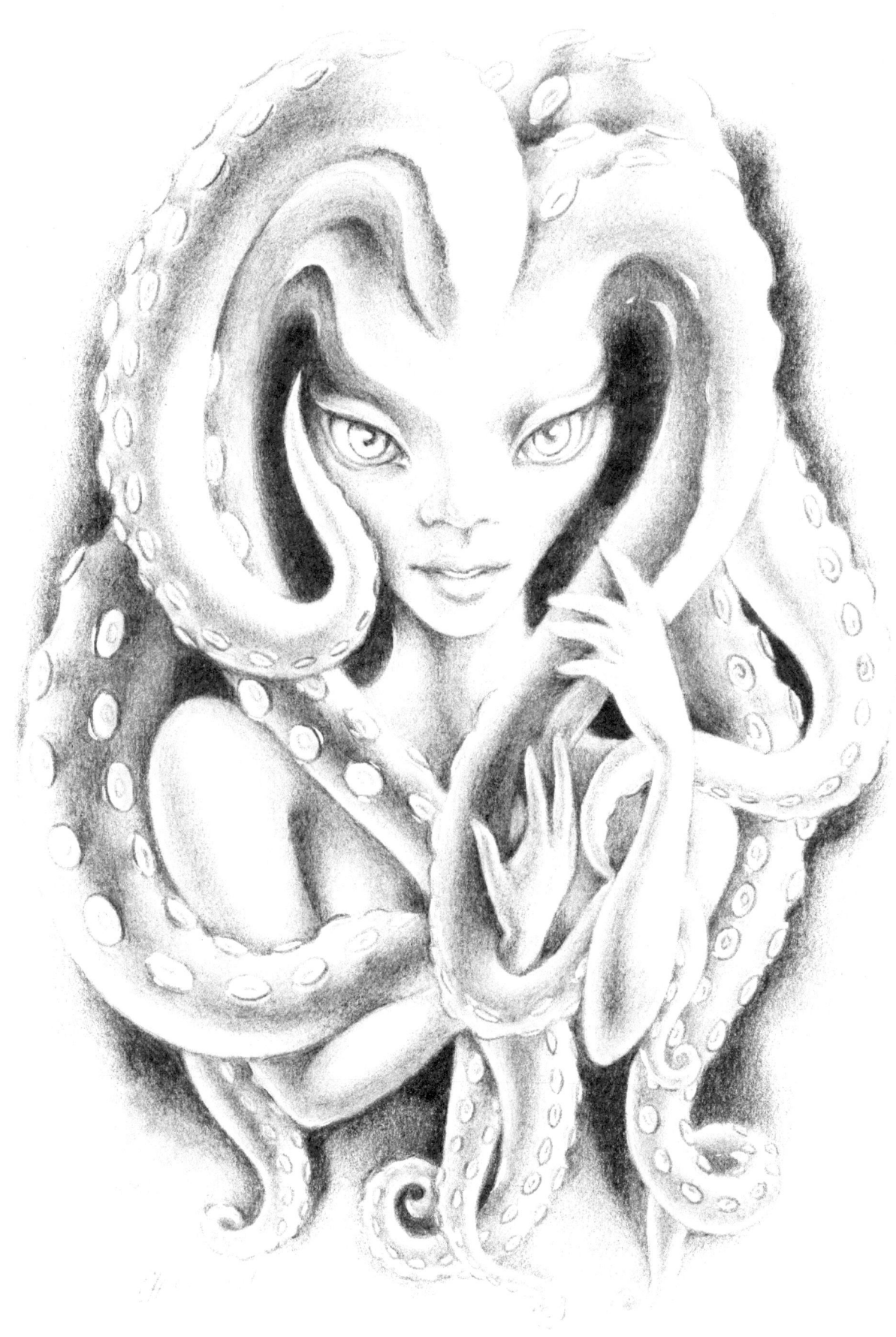

**CHARACTERS** *by Christine Karron*  *Ocean's Own*

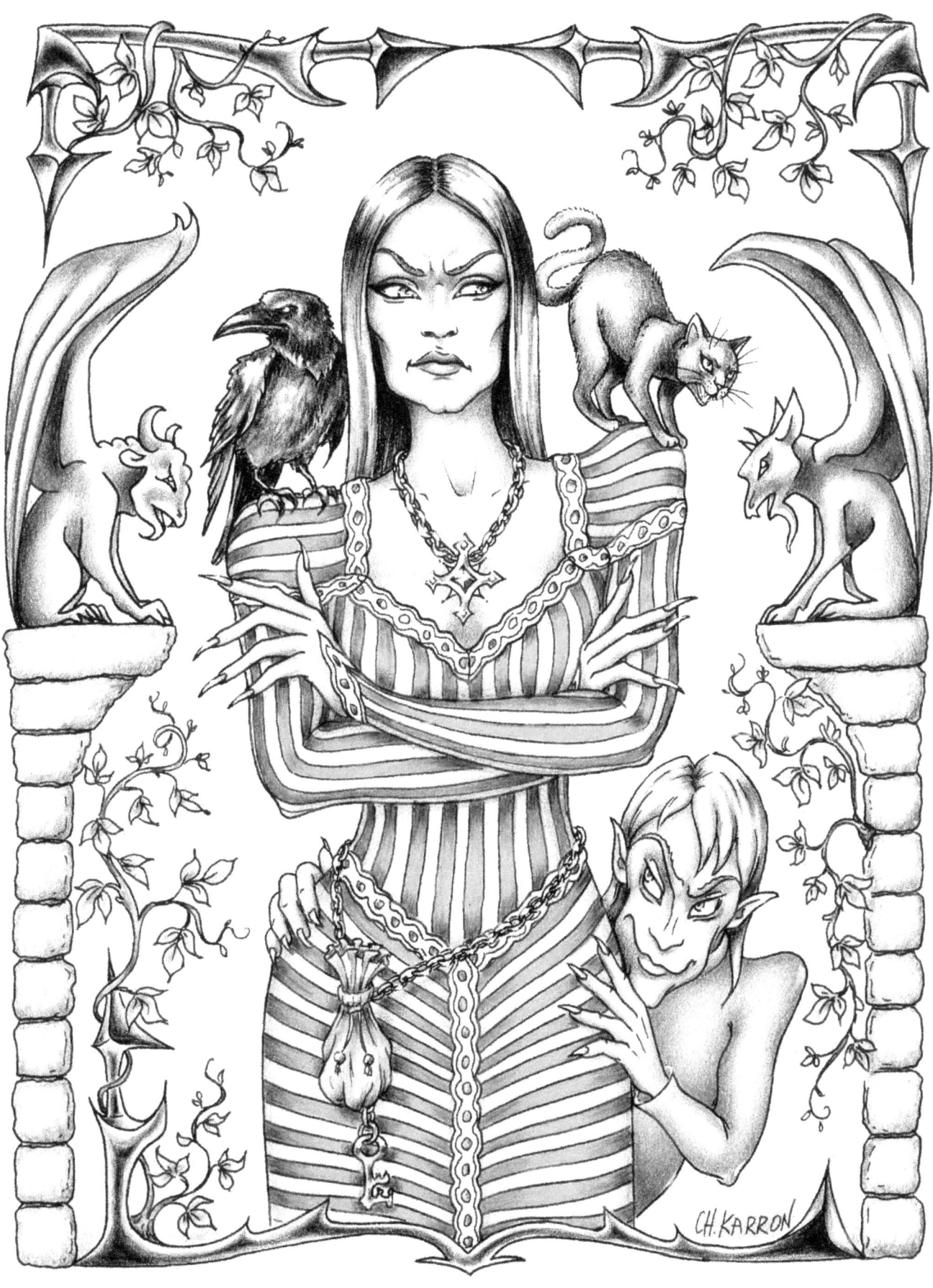

**CHARACTERS** by Christine Karron

Witch's Squad

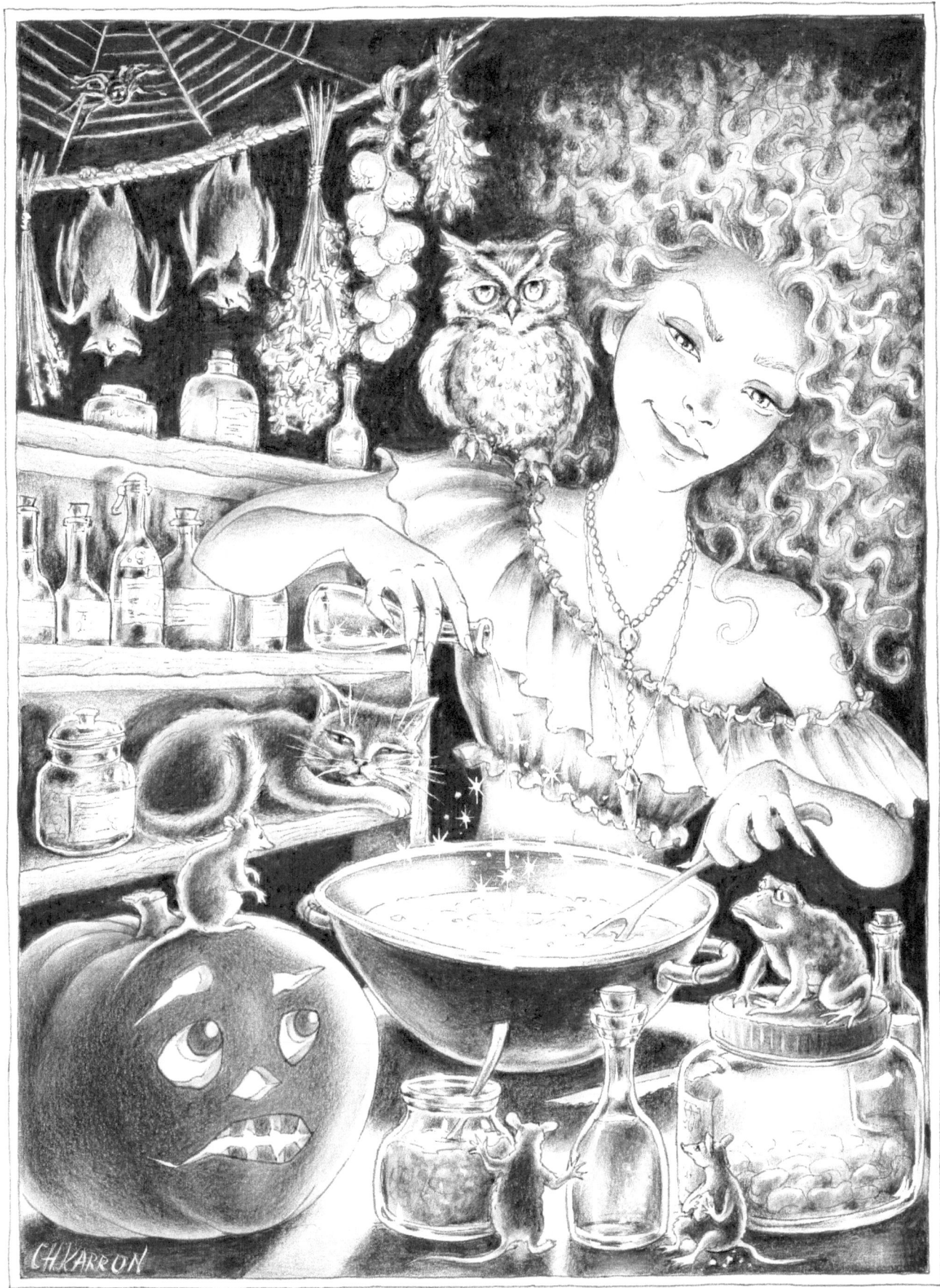

**CHARACTERS** by Christine Karron

*Shot of Magic*

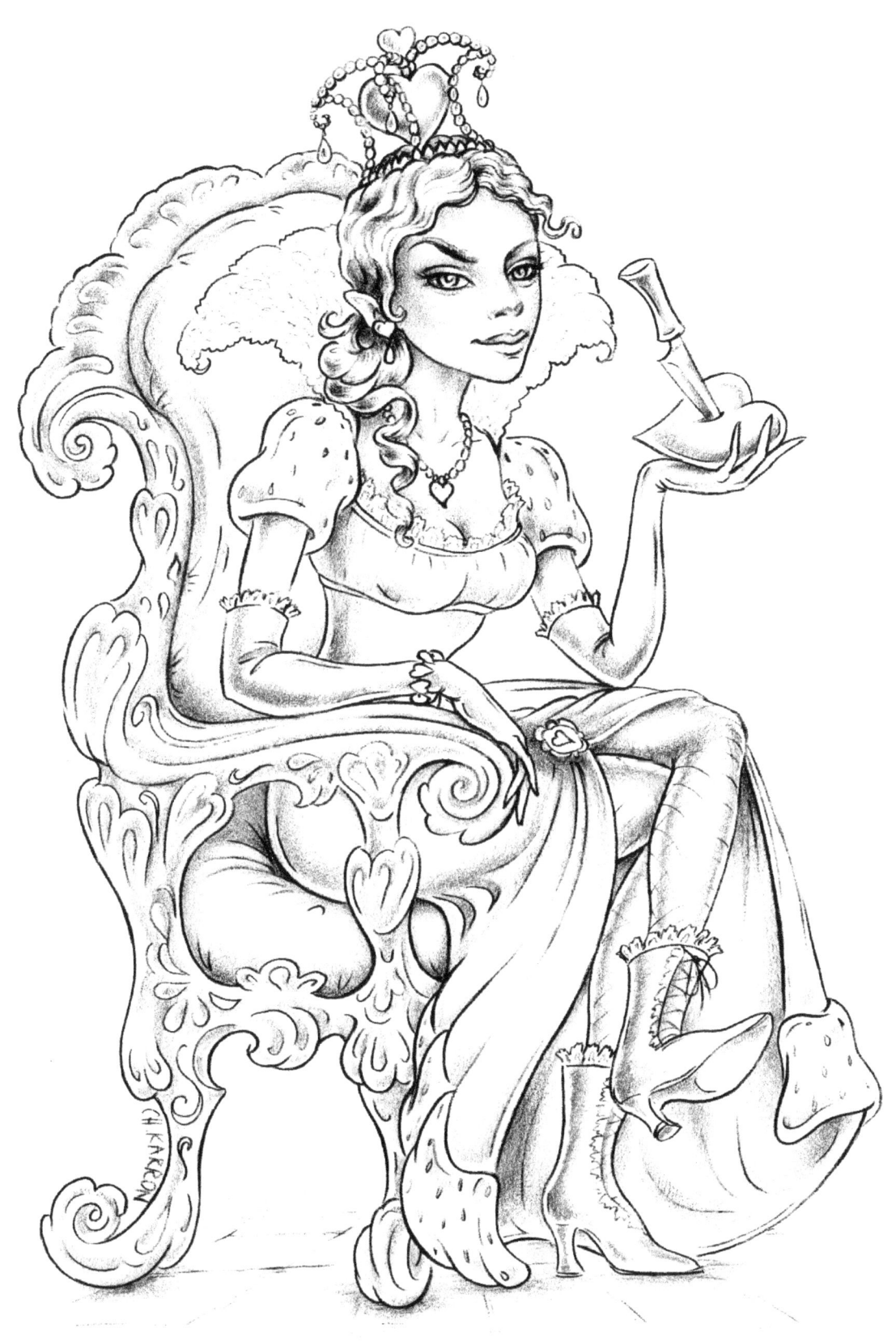

CHARACTERS by Christine Karron

Queen of Hearts

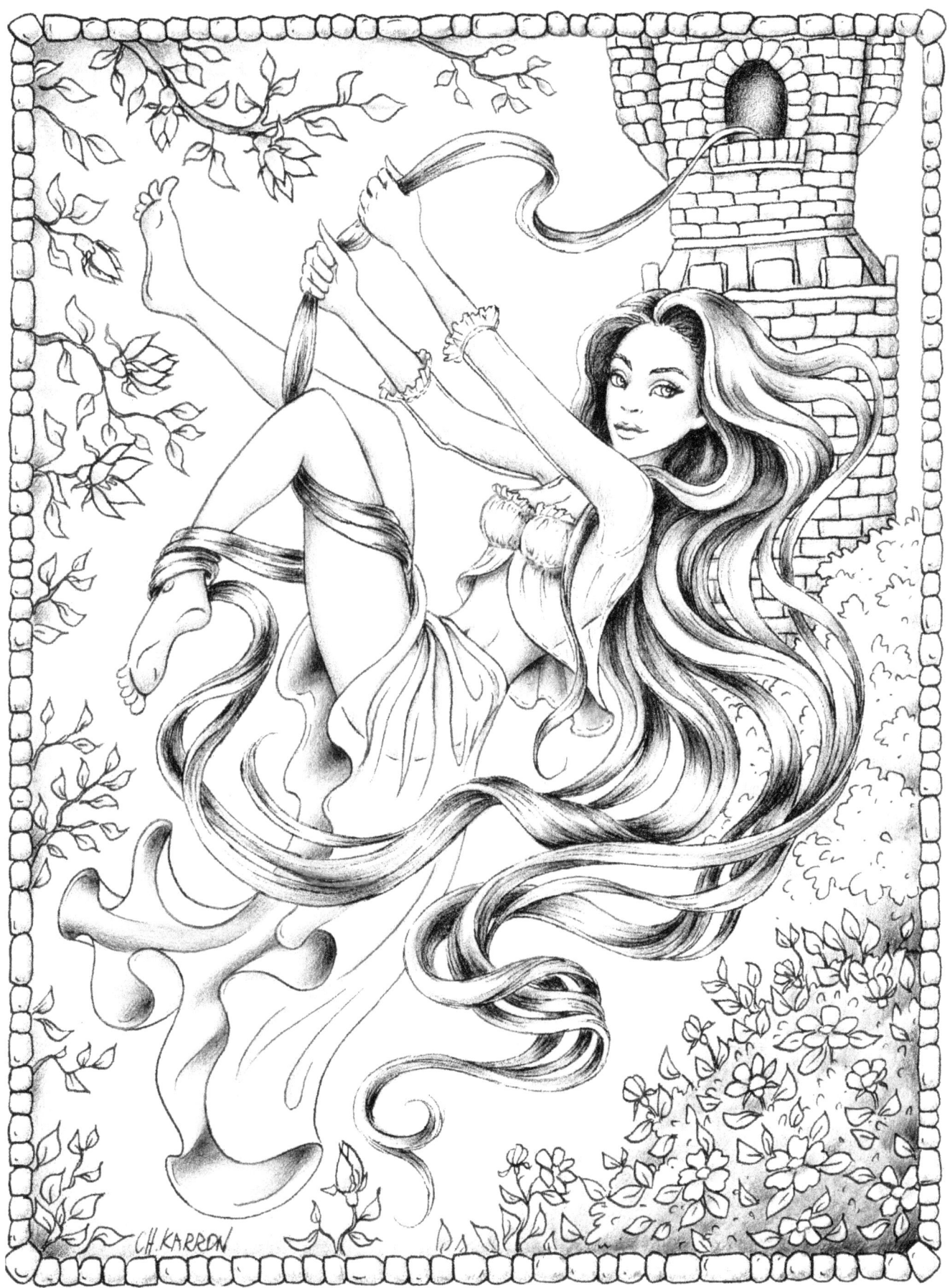

**CHARACTERS** *by Christine Karron*  Rapunzel

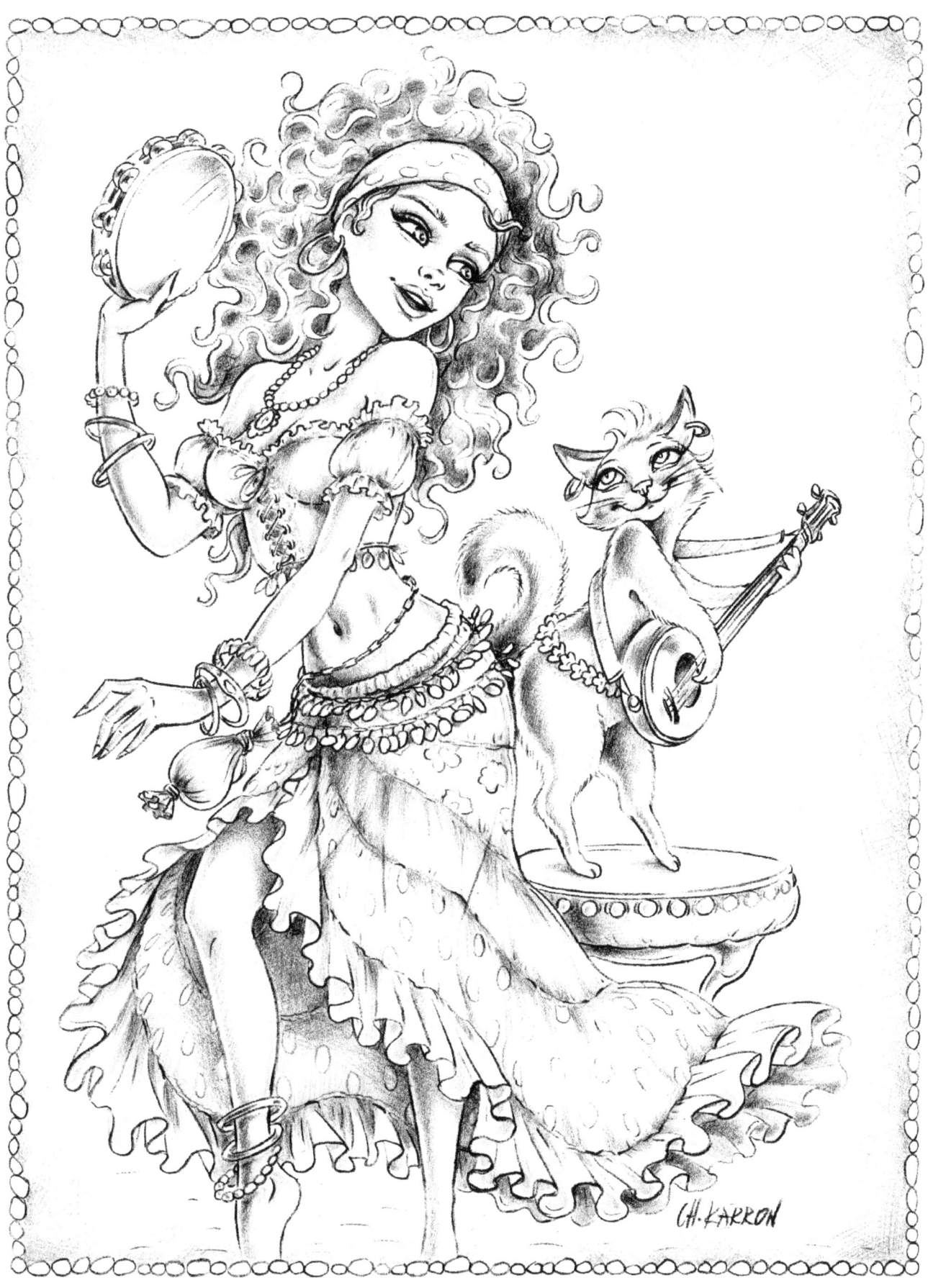

**CHARACTERS** by Christine Karron

*Gypsy Girls*

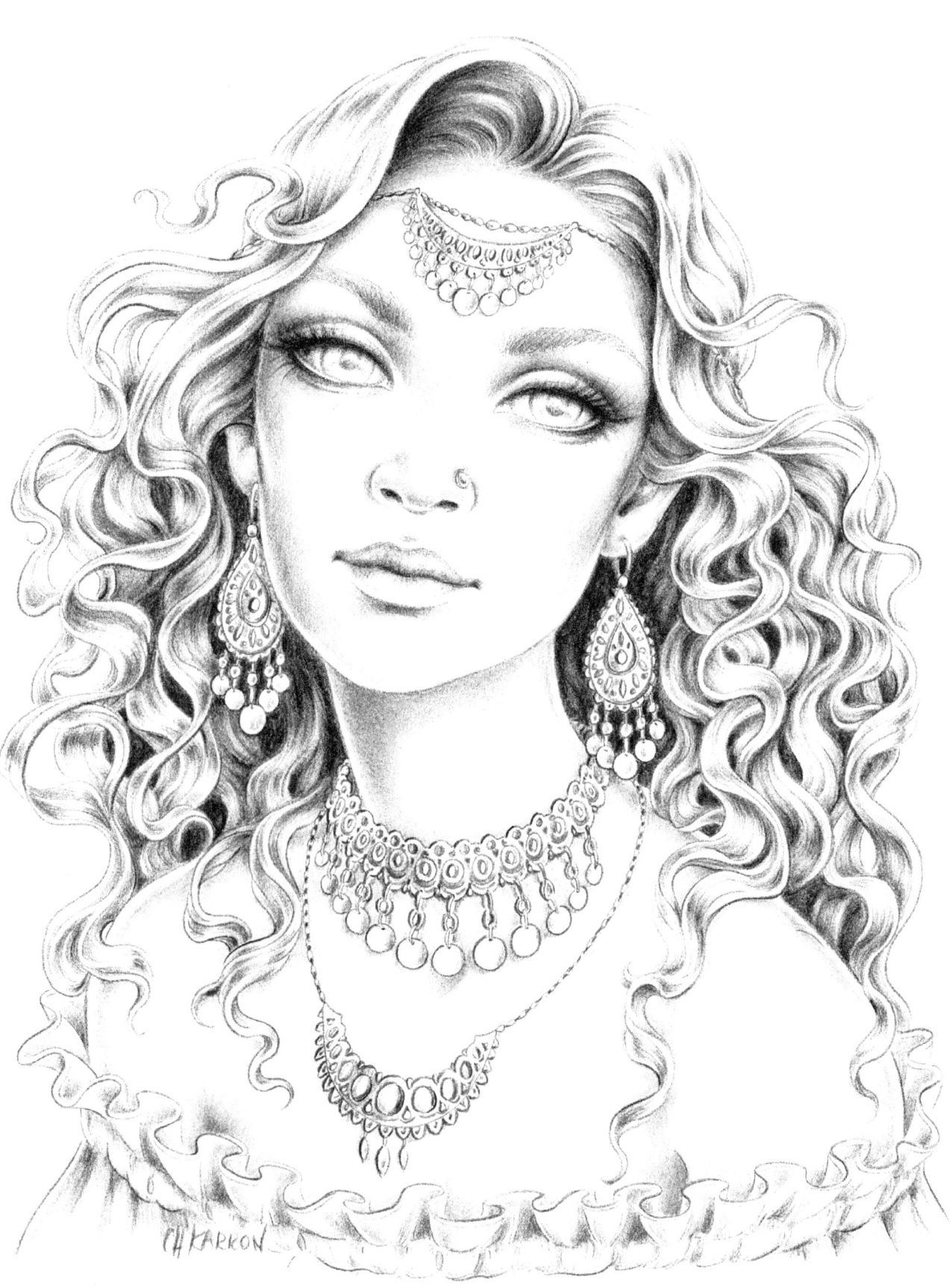

CHARACTERS by Christine Karron

Esmeralda

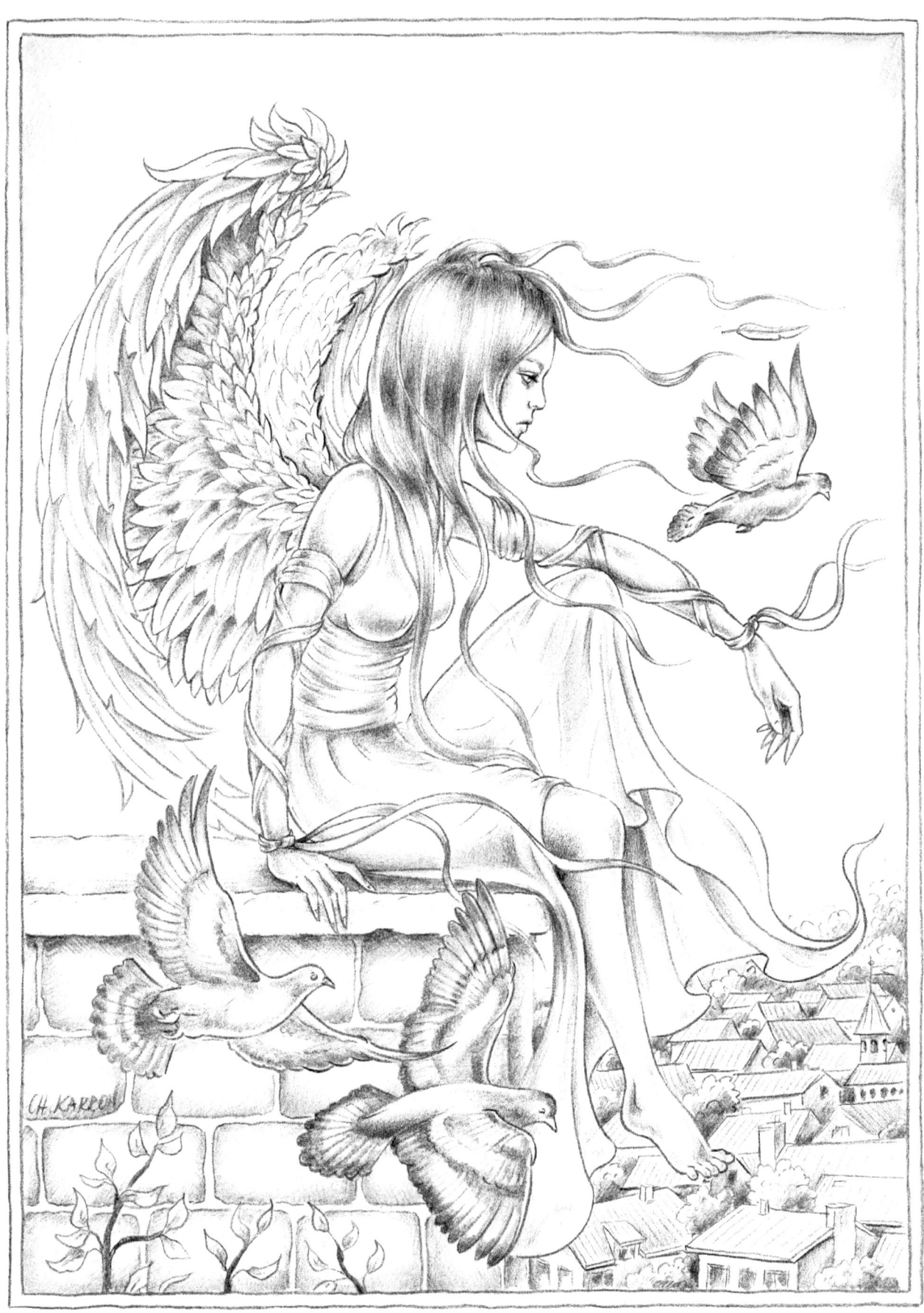

**CHARACTERS** by Christine Karron

*Over the Rooftops*

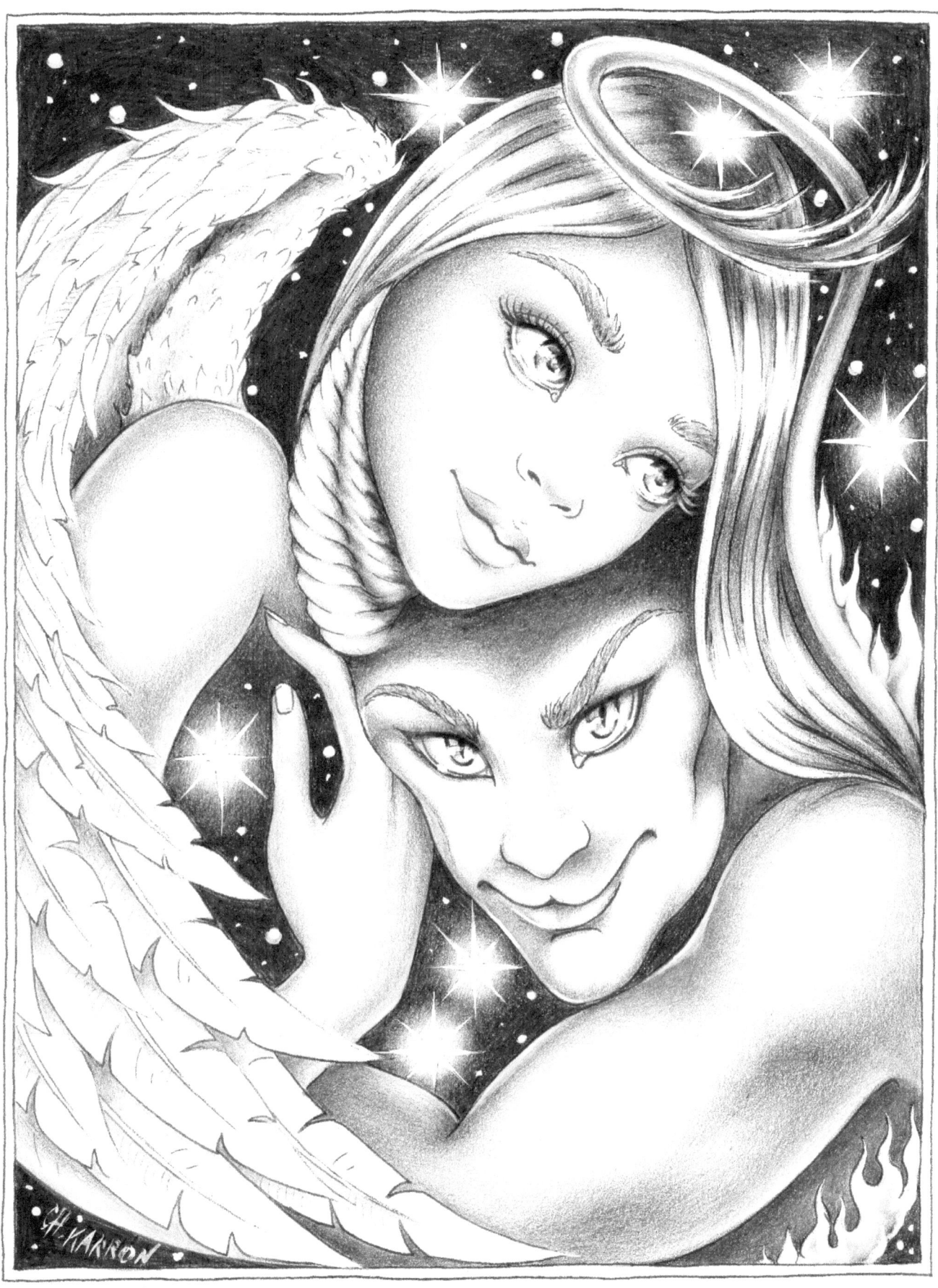

**CHARACTERS** by Christine Karron  *Good and Evil*

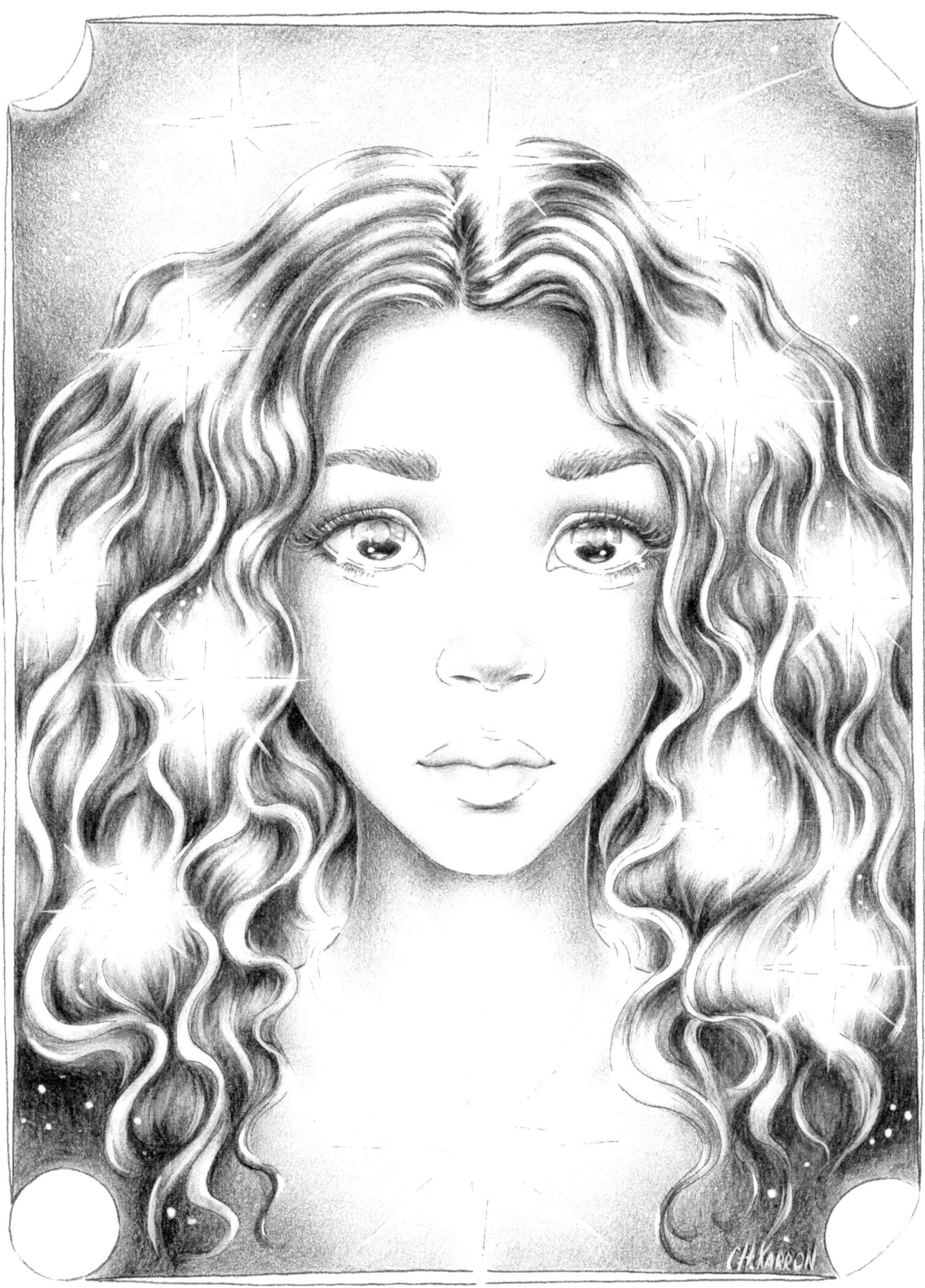

**CHARACTERS** by Christine Karron

*Starborn*

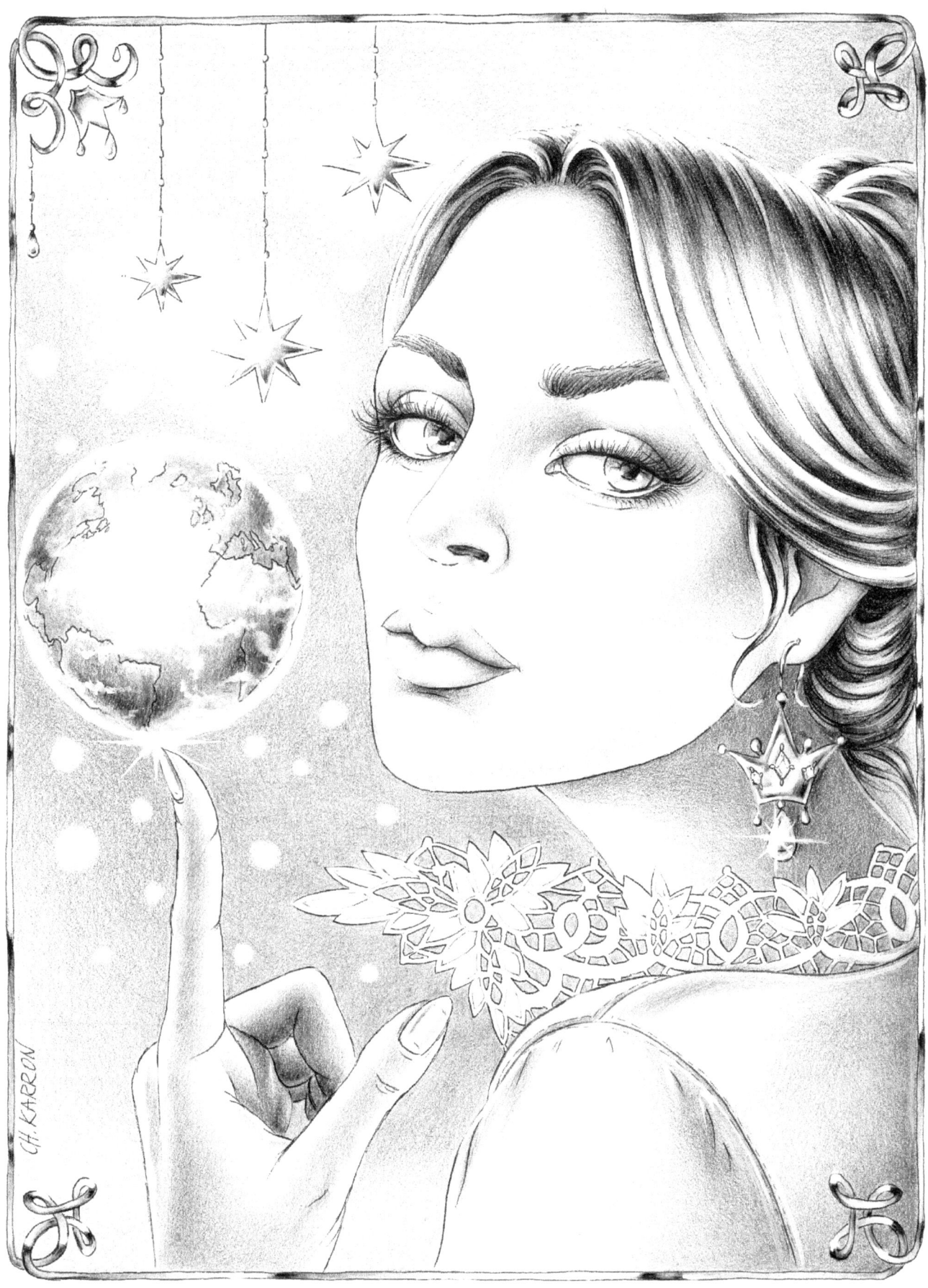

**CHARACTERS** *by Christine Karron*  *Queen of Her World*

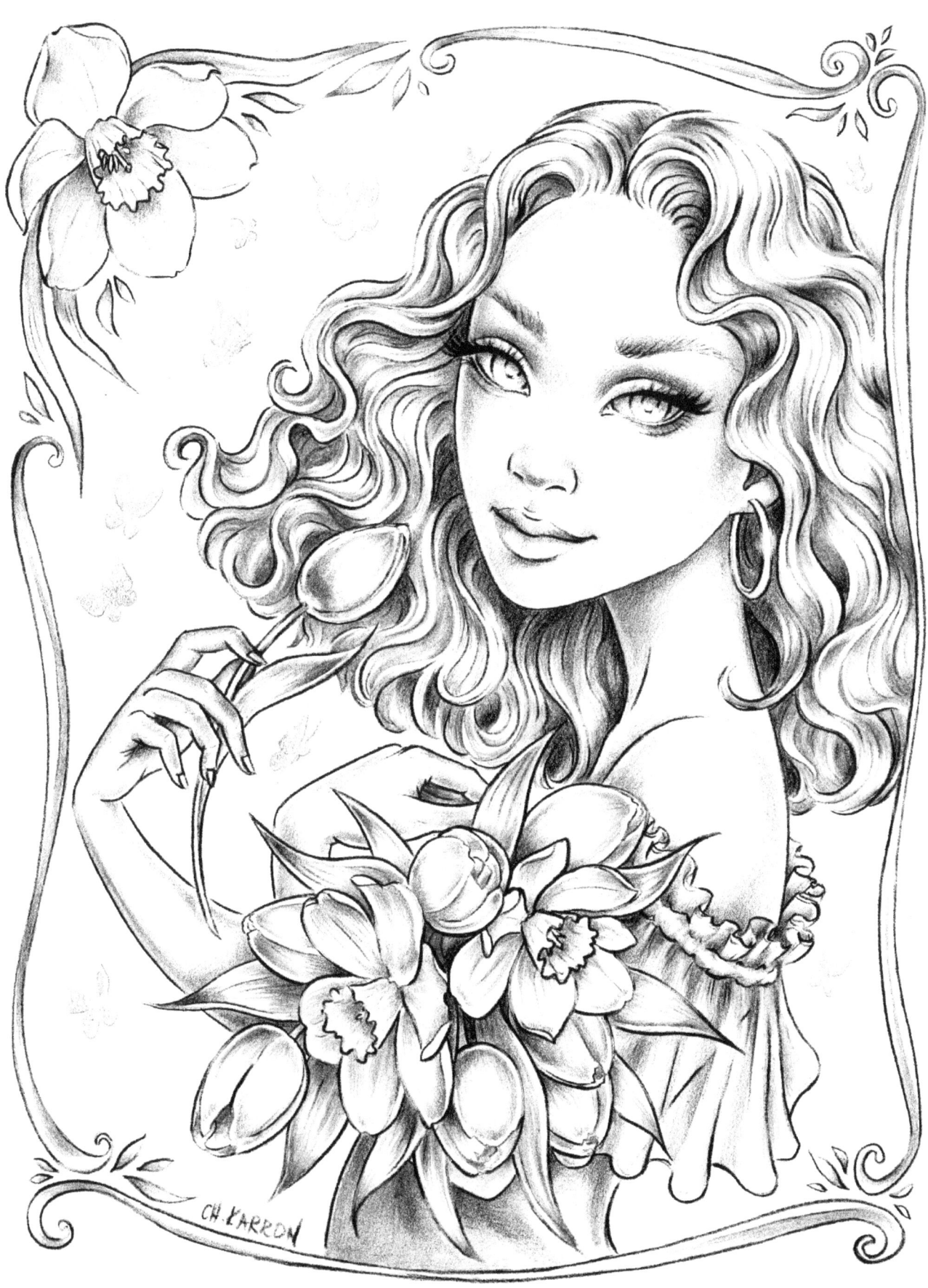

CHARACTERS *by Christine Karron*  *Scent of Spring*

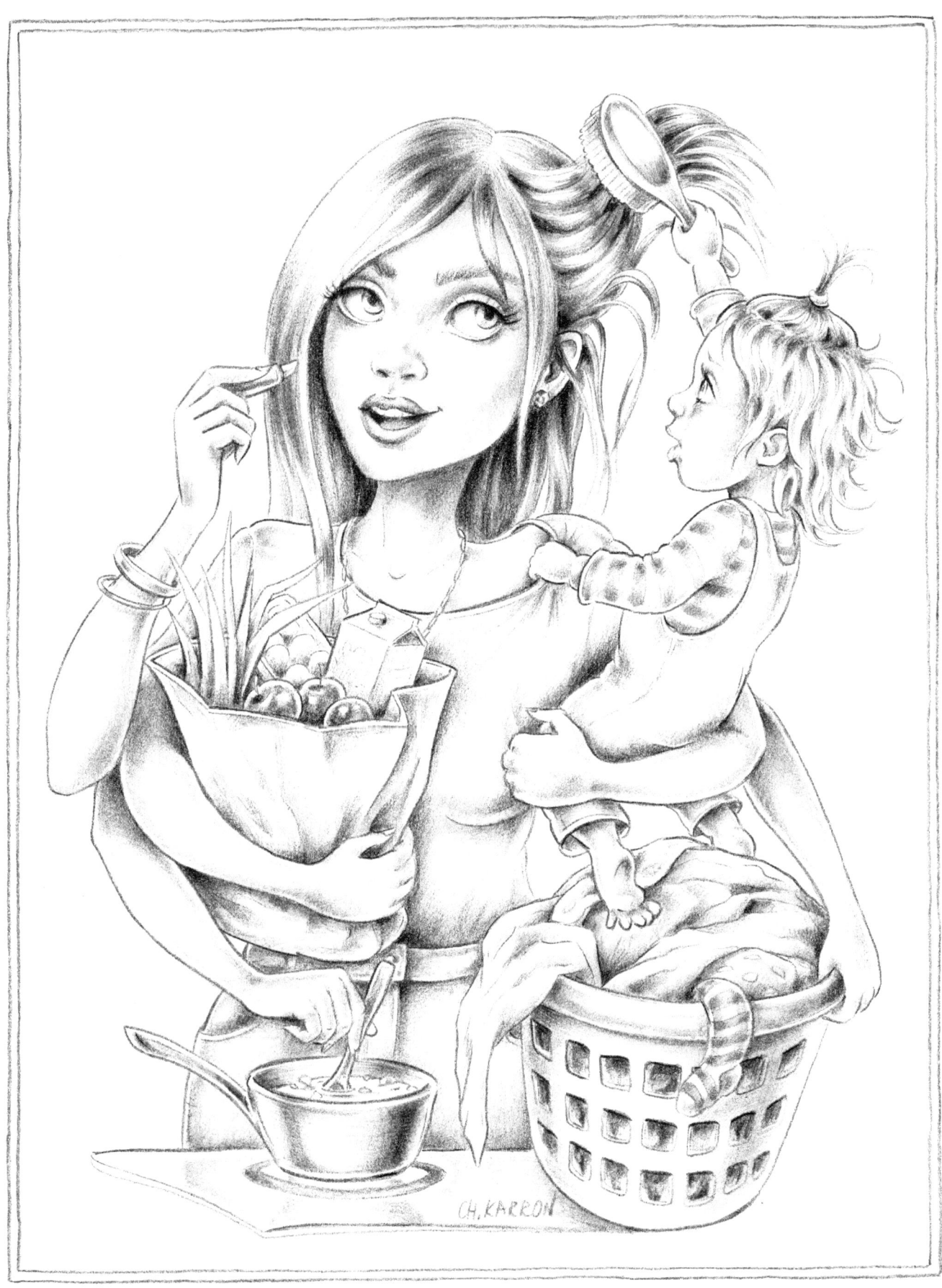

**CHARACTERS** *by Christine Karron* — *Mother's Day*

Also available

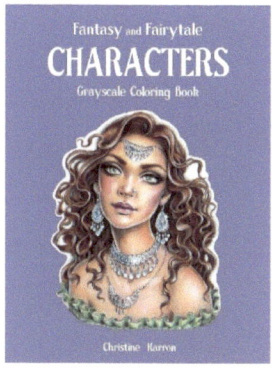
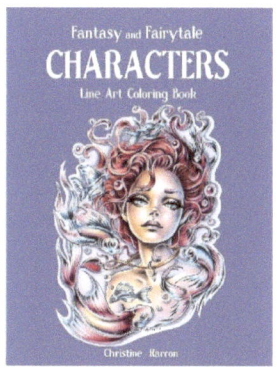
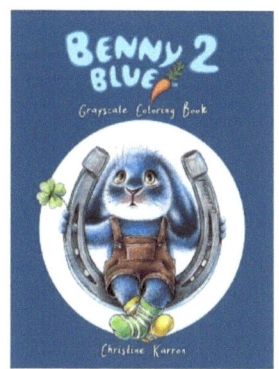
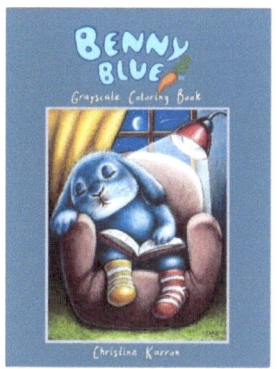
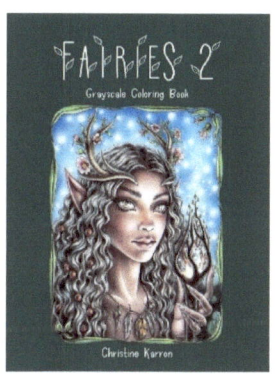
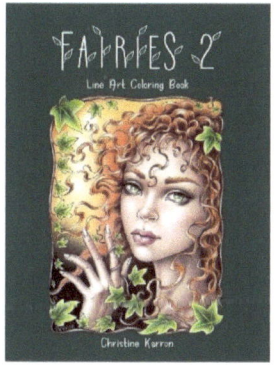
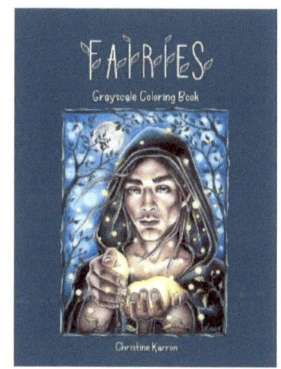
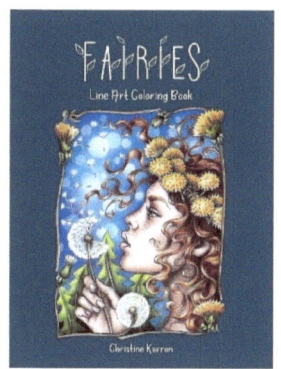
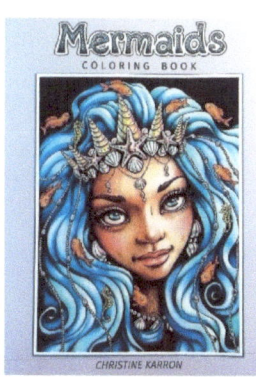
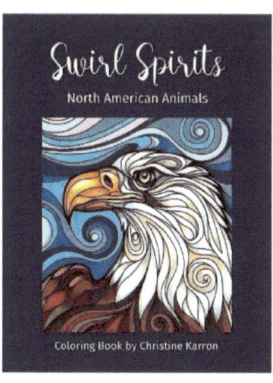
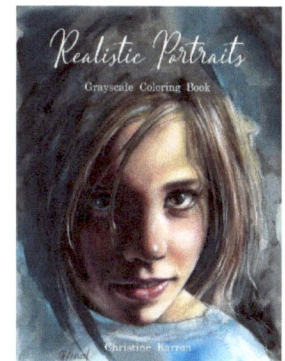

Christine Karron is an artist and illustrator based in Alberta, Canada.
Drawing and painting has always been Christine's passion.
With some formal training, self-education and experience,
between raising kids and taking care of her family,
Christine has been working as a freelance artist for 20 years now.

Christine has illustrated 6 children's books and a few years ago
she started the adventure of self-publishing coloring books.
Christine loves to create fantasy illustrations and characters
with a whimsical, narrative and humorous touch.
Working traditionally, she uses primarily colored pencils,
ink pens/markers and watercolor on paper.

You can follow Christine Karron on Facebook, Instagram and Twitter.

Printable digital downloads (in PDF format) of coloring books and
single coloring pages are available in Christine Karron's Etsy shop.

You can join Christine's Patreon page for a monthly coloring page.

Visit www.chkarron.com for coloring ideas, samples and demo videos.

You are welcome to join Christine Karron Coloring Collection Fan Group on Facebook.

If sharing colored images online please credit the artist - Christine Karron
You can use hashtags #christinekarron and/or #chkarron
Please DO NOT share or post uncolored versions of the images from this book
on Facebook, Pinterest or any other sharing sites online.

All rights reserved by Christine Karron
www.chkarron.com

www.ingramcontent.com/pod-product-compliance
Lightning Source LLC
Chambersburg PA
CBHW051214220526
45473CB00003B/1029